Microlife
That Lives in Soil

Steve Parker

www.raintreepublishers.co.uk
Visit our website to find out more information about **Raintree** books.

To order:
☎ Phone 44 (0) 1865 888112
📄 Send a fax to 44 (0) 1865 314091
💻 Visit the Raintree bookshop at **www.raintreepublishers.co.uk** to browse our catalogue and order online.

MONKEY PUZZLE MEDIA LTD

Produced for Raintree by
Monkey Puzzle Media Ltd,
Gissing's Farm, Fressingfield,
Suffolk IP21 5SH, UK

First published in Great Britain by Raintree,
Halley Court, Jordan Hill, Oxford OX2 8EJ,
part of Harcourt Education.
Raintree is a registered trademark of Harcourt
Education Ltd.

Editorial: Katie Orchard
Design: Mayer Media Ltd
Picture Research: Lynda Lines and Frances Bailey
Artwork: Michael Posen
Production: Duncan Gilbert
Indexing: Jane Parker

Originated by Chroma Graphics (Overseas) Pte Ltd.
Printed and bound in China by
South China Printing Company

ISBN 1 844 43398 6
10 09 08 07 06
10 9 8 7 6 5 4 3 2 1

British Library Cataloguing in Publication Data
Parker, Steve
Microlife that lives in soil. – (The amazing world of
microlife)
1.Microorganisms – Juvenile literature
2.Soil microbiology – Juvenile literature
I.Title
579.1'757

Acknowledgements
The publishers would like to thank the following for
permission to reproduce photographs: Alamy p. **24**
(Nigel Cattlin/Holt Studios Int. Ltd.); Corbis pp. **28**
(Robert Pickett), **29** (Michael and Patricia Fogden);
Getty Images p. **5 top** (David Wolley/Stone);
photolibrary.com pp. **5 bottom** (David M. Dennis),
10; Rex Features p. **15** (Marja Airio); Science Photo
Library pp. **1** (VVG), **3** (VVG), **4** (Andrew Syred), **8**
(David Scharf), **11** (Dr. Jeremy Burgess), **12** (Dr. David
Patterson), **14** (Eye of Science), **16** (Laguna Design), **17**
(Andrew Syred), **18** (VVG), **19** (Andrew Syred), **21**
(VVG), **22** (Geoff Kidd), **26** (Andrew Syred), **27** (Peter
Chadwick); Still Pictures pp. **7** (Kelvin Aitken), **25**
(Gayo); Topfoto pp. **6** (T. Balabhadkan/UNEP) **9** (Bob
Daemmrich/The Image Works), **13** (Bob Daemmrich/
The Image Works), **20** (Roberto Matassa).

Cover photograph of a velvet mite reproduced with
permission of Science Photo Library (Eye of Science).

Every effort has been made to contact copyright
holders of any material reproduced in this book. Any
omissions will be rectified in subsequent printings if
notice is given to the publishers.

The paper used to print this book comes from
sustainable resources.

Contents

Any words appearing in bold, **like this,** are explained
in the Glossary.

Micro-jungle!

Every time you visit a garden or park, you tread on a micro-jungle! The soil under your feet is wriggling with living things. We can easily see some of them, such as earthworms and **grubs**. Others are too small for our own eyes to see. But we can make them look much bigger, using magnifying glasses and **microscopes**.

A microscope can make this mite look as big as your hand. In real life, it is only as big as this full stop.

A magnifying glass makes minibeasts like this earthworm look much bigger than they really are.

Why we need soil

Soil with plenty of microlife in it is rich, or **fertile**. It has everything a plant needs to stay healthy and grow. Grass, vegetables, fruits, and crops such as wheat are all plants. If there was no micro-jungle in the soil, plants could not grow, and we would be very hungry!

Rich and poor soil

There are many kinds of soil. Rich, or **fertile**, soil has plenty of plants growing in it. Grass and trees grow well because the soil is home to lots of microlife. All living things need water, food and fresh air to help them grow. Fertile soil with plenty of air holes in it has all these things, and so is full of life.

Good and bad

Other kinds of soil are not fertile. They are poor soils, which have little microlife and few plants. Soils become poor because they lack water and are too dry. They may have few **nutrients** (goodness) as food. Some soil is too squashed together, with no air spaces in it, so plant roots cannot grow there.

If soil becomes very dry and cracked, the microlife that lives there will die.

Good soil is damp and crumbly. It has plenty of tiny spaces for air and water, and lots of nutrients.

WHAT IS HUMUS?
Rich soil has plenty of **humus** – bits and pieces of dead plants and animals. They rot and break up, slowly turning into new soil. Humus provides lots of nutrients, which microlife and plants use as food.

Micro-bugs

The tiniest living things in soil are called **bacteria**. One handful of soil contains millions of bacteria. Some soil bacteria grow like plants, using light from the Sun to make their own food. They can live only near the surface, where there is enough light. Other kinds of bacteria do not need light. They feed on the **nutrients** in soil.

Soil bacteria have many different shapes, such as rods, sticks and balls.

Gardening is fun. But we should cover cuts and grazes safely, to stop harmful bacteria from the soil getting into our bodies.

How bacteria help

Bacteria help make soil rich and **fertile**. They help to rot (break down) **humus**. This provides food for larger plants and animals. Bacteria are also eaten by tiny animals in the soil.

CARE WITH SOIL
Some kinds of soil bacteria can be harmful and cause serious illness. We should never put soil in our mouths, and we should always wash our hands properly after touching soil.

Micro-plants

Many kinds of plants, such as stinging nettles, flowers and trees, grow up from the soil. Other plants grow inside the soil, too. Most of these plants are so tiny that they look like specks of green powder or even green slime!

Algae are tiny plants that live in soil. They do not have roots, stems and flowers, like big plants. They are mostly shaped like tiny green pieces of string.

Light and water

Just like big plants, micro-plants need light from the Sun. They live on the surface of the soil or just underneath, where the light can reach them. These micro-plants also need water. They grow in the very thin layer of water that covers the tiny grains of soil. Micro-plants in soil are eaten by all kinds of tiny creatures. These tiny creatures are then eaten by bigger ones, and so on.

As these puddles dry up, they leave micro-plants around their edges, which look like coloured powder or slime.

SMALL AND BIG
Most micro-plants in soil are called algae. Much bigger kinds of algae grow on the seashore – we call these large algae seaweeds.

Sliding along

What wobbles like jelly as it moves through soil? The answer is an **amoeba**. The amoeba belongs to a group of tiny living things called **protists**. The amoeba eats smaller microlife such as **bacteria**.

When the soil dries out, some amoebas make a see-through shell and wait until it rains.

NO MOUTH

Amoebas eat things like bacteria. An amoeba does not have a mouth. It feeds by sliding over bacteria, covering them, and taking them into its jelly-like body.

Other protists

There are many other kinds of soil protists, too. Some are shaped like sausages or cushions, with a long thread sticking out. A protist waves this thread about, to push itself through the soil.

There are millions of protists in a bucket of soil. Some are green and grow like plants, using the Sun's light to make their food. All these protists are food for slightly bigger hunters in the soil.

If soil gets too dry, the microlife will die. There will not be enough food for the bigger plants and animals, and they will die, too. This is why we sometimes need to water our gardens.

Recycling soil

In damp weather, mushrooms and toadstools grow on soil. These kinds of living things are called **fungi**. Fungi cause rot and **decay**. They break dead plants and animals into tiny pieces, which crumble and soak back into the soil. Fungi grow tiny threads into the soil, which turn old bits of plants and animals into a 'soup'. The fungi then soak up the soup as their food.

The tiny threads of a fungus form a tangled net in the soil.

Mushrooms and toadstools grow up from much smaller threads hidden in the soil.

How fungi spread

Threads of fungi sometimes bunch together and grow upwards, to form a mushroom or toadstool. The mushroom's top, or cap, makes millions of powder-like specks called **spores**. Spores float away in the wind. If they land in a suitable damp place, they grow into a new fungus.

NATURAL RECYCLING

Fungi are nature's way of recycling. If they did not cause rot and decay, dead bits of plants and animals would pile up and soon cover us!

15

Tiny creatures

What's the smallest animal in soil? You may think of a baby earthworm, but some creatures are far tinier. One is called a wheel-animal. It has a mouth at one end with tiny hairs around it, in a ring or wheel shape. Another tiny soil creature is the water-bear. As it walks along on its stumpy legs, it looks like a tiny bear.

A wheel-animal has a tiny body shaped like a vase or funnel, with no legs.

BACK TO LIFE

Wheel-animals and water-bears live in the water in soil. If the soil dries out, they can still survive. When the soil gets wet again, they come back to life.

Micro-hunters

Wheel-animals and water-bears live in the very thin layer of water around pieces of soil. Wheel-animals eat anything smaller than themselves, such as micro-plants and micro-bugs. Water-bears suck the juices out of plants. In turn, both of these tiny creatures are eaten by bigger soil animals.

The water-bear has a head, a plump body and eight short, fat legs.

Soil mites

If we look closely at the ground, we may see a small spider running across the soil. We know it is a spider because it has eight legs. The spider could be hunting for an even smaller creature, which also has eight legs. This is the type of tiny soil animal called a mite.

In real life, this mite is only as big as this full stop. But it can tear its victims apart and suck up their juices.

Small and smaller

There are many different kinds of soil mites. Some are as big as this 'o'. Others are a hundred times smaller. The tiniest kinds eat whatever they find, mainly bits of dead plants and animals. Bigger mites have strong mouths shaped like pincers. They hunt all kinds of smaller creatures, including other mites.

fangs

One of the mite's main enemies is the centipede. It stabs its live food, or **prey**, with its very long, tooth-like **fangs**.

Pincers and springs

In a spadeful of soil, you can easily see creatures like earthworms. Look more closely and you might see little specks moving. These are tiny animals that live in the soil. One type is the false-scorpion. It has pincers like a real scorpion, and eight legs. Another type is the springtail. It has a head with eyes and two bendy feelers, and a long body with six legs.

NO STING

A false-scorpion looks like a tiny version of a real scorpion – except that it has no tail, and so it cannot sting.

Many tiny creatures hide in **leaf litter** – the layer of old leaves, twigs and other bits and pieces on top of soil.

Under the springtail's tail is a Y-shaped part which can flick down very fast, to make the springtail leap into the air.

Different lifestyles

Springtails and false-scorpions live in very different ways. Most springtails eat any small bits and pieces of food they can find. Most false-scorpions are fierce hunters. But in the soil, all of them become food for larger creatures.

Grubby grubs

Many kinds of creatures spend all their lives underground. But some stay in the soil only while they are young. Many are the young of insects, called **grubs**. The soil is their nursery. As they change into grown-up insects, they come to the surface and run or fly away!

STAGES IN GROWING UP

The grub or young form of an insect is called a **larva**. It wriggles and feeds. Then it grows a hard case and becomes a **pupa**, which lies still. Then the pupa hatches into the grown-up insect.

The leatherjacket lives in the soil for a year or more, before it changes into the grown-up cranefly.

cranefly pupa

adult cranefly

cranefly larva
(leatherjacket)
in soil

cranefly
eggs

A cranefly egg hatches into a larva. The larva turns into a pupa. When the pupa splits open, an adult cranefly comes out.

Grubs to grown-ups

One of these grubs is the leatherjacket. It is brown and it eats plant roots. It wriggles like a **maggot** because it has no legs. After a time it grows a hard case, or 'jacket', around itself. When the case splits open, a cranefly or daddy-long-legs, comes out and flies away across the soil.

Soil pests

In wild areas, there are many different kinds of plants and animals. But in farming, the land is used to raise just one type of crop. A huge field of one kind of plant, such as potatoes, is like a giant feast for certain kinds of soil creatures. These creatures feed well and breed faster than they would in a natural area. They soon become **pests**.

This young, or **maggot**, of the cabbage-root fly is hiding in a plant stem. Millions of these maggots can soon destroy a field of cabbages.

Too much food

One type of pest is the wireworm – the young of the click-beetle. It nibbles crops such as wheat. Various kinds of mites can become pests, too, as they eat vegetables growing in the soil. Eelworms also eat their way into vegetables and plant roots. These tiny soil creatures can ruin a field of crops in weeks.

SOIL PESTS
Around the world, about one-tenth of all the food that farmers grow in fields is eaten or ruined by animal pests.

Farmers often spray their crops with chemicals to kill pests.

Underground cities

Big cities can be very busy. There are always many people rushing about. The places where minibeasts such as ants and termites live in the soil are like cities, too. These tiny insects dig tunnels all day and night. They move grains of soil with their pincer-like mouths. Thousands of them work together to make a nest of burrows and chambers in the soil.

BIGGEST CITIES
Termites make the biggest cities of any animal. There might be more than 10 million termites in one huge nest.

In a busy nest, ants 'talk' to each other by tapping their feelers together.

Always working

One special ant or termite in each underground city is the queen, who lays eggs. The rest are workers. Some make new tunnels and repair old ones, while others collect food. Some keep the eggs clean and feed the young. There are soldiers, too. Soldier ants and termites fight enemies, from small ant-eating spiders to the huge anteater!

Termites build a huge mound or tower of hard, dry mud above their nest in the cool, damp soil.

Nature's gardeners

Almost every patch of soil has long, thin and wriggly worms. Some of them are quite large, and can be longer than your finger. These are earthworms. Other worms are too small to see. They are called roundworms.

Some worms, such as this common earthworm, eat soil. Others feed on tiny creatures or suck juices from plant roots.

NATURE'S GARDENERS

Earthworms are sometimes called 'nature's gardeners'. As they tunnel, they mix up the soil and spread out the nutrients. It is like a gardener digging soil – although much slower!

Tasty soil!

Worms do not just live in soil, they eat it! The worm takes in the nutrients (goodness) from the soil. Then it gets rid of what it does not need through its tail end, as squiggles of soft mud, called worm casts. As worms eat, they make tunnels, which let light, air and water into the soil. Worms also pull into their tunnels old leaves and bits of plants, which rot and **decay**. Worms are very good for soil.

Millipedes feed on old and dead leaves. Sometimes they hide from their enemies in worm tunnels.

Find out for yourself

Books to read

First Discovery: Under the Ground, Pascale De Bourgoing and Daniele Bour (Scholastic, 1995)

Jump Into Science: Dirt, Steve Tomecek and Nancy Woodman (Illustrator) (National Geographic Children's, 2002)

Nature Upclose: An Earthworm's Life, John Himmelman (Children's Press, 2001)

Under One Rock: Bugs, Slugs, and Other Ughs, Anthony D. Fredericks and Jennifer Dirubbio (Dawn Publications, 2001)

Using the internet

Explore the Internet to find out more about microlife that lives in soil. Websites can change, so if the links below no longer work, do not worry. Use a search engine, such as **www.yahooligans.com** or **www.internet4kids.com**, and type in a keyword such as fungus, mite, rotifer or humus, or the name of a particular type of microlife.

Websites

http://school.discovery.com/schooladventures/soil/index.html
Exploring what's in soil, including the many creatures that live there, plus a soil safari game that shrinks you down to microsize.

www.fieldmuseum.org/ua/
An underground adventure looking at soil, including an animated virtual trip into this dark, damp, secret world and what you would see if you were one centimetre tall.